Dedication

I would like to dedicate this book to my brother for his encouragement to pursue filing of disability.

Acknowledgements

The Internet for its abundance of information available on this subject and to the SSA and DDS employees I interacted with. You are kind beyond words.

Index

Introduction

Let me first say that I am writing this book to help the thousands of people that may be lost when facing the daunting task of applying for disability with the Social Security Administration. It is a very time consuming and frustrating process for those that do not take the time to learn the correct steps to take or even not to take. I hope you find this book helpful as it is a firsthand account of my story and how I was able to be successful in just 32 days.

Chapter One

Let me first give a little background of my situation and how I came to the point of applying for disability. I have knee osteoarthritis in both knees and have suffered with knee stiffness and pain that has gradually worsened over the years. I never considered the possibility of disability even though I had finally reached a point that standing more than a few minutes was unbearable and walking was the same. Although sitting was obviously better I would become extremely stiff in a very short time. I lived with the chronic pain for a long time and had cortisone injections, gel injections and my Orthopedist said only knee replacements in both knees would solve this. I have only known a few people that had this done and none of them seemed to be better off after their surgery so I am reluctant to have this done and also because of the cost. I still never believed disability to be anything other than loss of limb, eyesight, being paralyzed, etc. But then one day I happened across a Facebook post about disability, probably an ad for a Lawyer, but it prompted me to start researching online. I ended up finding the steps that are used to determine eligibility and learned if you had a "listed" condition it was automatic. Well, there it was "narrowing of the joint space". I thought, I have no space as I am bone on bone. I read it over and over and it seemed like I was eligible and so now began the research. But first, let me paint the picture of my overall health. I am 57 years old, 350 pounds, 6'0" tall. I had an abnormal heartbeat a few years prior, type 2 diabetes, Melanoma 12 years before, sleep apnea, had an episode of vasculitis. I doubt that all of these things were factors in being approved for disability but I figured why not throw everything in.

Chapter Two

I did research just like I am sure all of you are doing with the exception that I have a very specific capacity to analyze in great detail and see the big picture. I immersed myself on Google looking at every possible thing that looked like it would help me. There is an immense amount of information from Lawyers on videos and it was the greatest source of information. I put in hours and hours of looking over videos, different websites, and the Social Security Disability website reviewing the "process". All of the information that is available on the internet is very valuable and is easy to find just search for anything to do with disability and you will find an abundance. Now the downside is just about everything you will read is going to tell you that almost all claims are denied on the initial application. I found almost no stories or information that talked about success. It seemed that most people feel like it is mandated to the Social Security Administration to deny. This was

Lawyers, individuals, web sites, even my own Lawyer. I should mention at this point I did not use a Lawyer. I have a LegalShield membership and I called and was advised to apply first in person and it will likely be denied and then call them back for representation. I never called them back as I was approved the first try. I was extremely worried about being denied and going to appeal because I was living off of my savings and had not worked for a year. most everything I read talked about the appeal process taking a year to get a hearing and I knew I would not have enough money to last that long. Now one of the first things I learned is that for the Lawyers fee it is common practice that they don't get involved until the appeal process and their fees come out of your back pay and is limited by law to $6000.00 or 25% of the back pay whichever is lower. You do not pay anything up front. If you don't win your case, you pay nothing. So obviously a Lawyer will likely not take your case unless he/she feels like you have a good chance of winning. Regardless of whether you get denied or not I recommend you sign up for LegalShield. It is only about $20 bucks a month and is well worth having your own law firm for many reasons. You can get it by going to www.legalshield.com/hub/kthomas83. So now on to the steps I took to get approved on my initial application in 32 days.

Chapter Three

Call Social Security and get an appointment. Have a notepad handy as you will be told what to bring. Their number is 1-800-772-1213 M-F 7am to 7pm. I was told where and when to go. What I was told to bring:

Actual prescription meds, not a list but the actual bottles of medicine.

Ex-spouse name and date of birth

Medical records

Birth Certificate

Deed to home

Make and model of cars

Current bank statement

Life insurance policies

Last year W2

I was instructed to go to a website and print the application and fill it out and bring it with me to the appointment. Now to jump ahead just a bit I had some confusion that may or may not have been to my advantage. I hand wrote out the application that I had printed just to make sure I had it filled out correctly and when I was satisfied I had done the best I could I went online to the application and typed everything so it would be legible. At the very end there was a medical release form and I wasn't sure if I was supposed to submit that or not so I called the SSA again and was told that yes fill out the form online and submit. That way they would have all the information when I went to my appointment. I said great and did just that. It turns out she told me wrong and what I now had done was applied online and I still had my earlier appointment. Now here is what I suggest. You do exactly the same thing. Get your appointment set up, get your application filled out (which I will detail in the next steps) then submit online. I can't say if this made a difference but why chance it.

Chapter Four

Call and get every medical record you can. You need this from every single doctor you have seen in the last couple of years. What you want is documented proof of any and all conditions you have. You need to have the records so you can obtain dates and details for filling out your application. You will need to call the doctors first and tell them what you want. I had to go there and sign a release to pick them up. I was able to get all of mine with the exception of my past primary care doctor that was going to take longer than the time before my SSA appointment. I did have my current primary doctors though. You will need to move quickly on this because when you call SSA your appointment will be in about two weeks. Hopefully during your doctor visits you have let them know about your pain and how it is affecting you. I was very shocked my medical records from my orthopedist did not mention difficulty of stiffness when sitting for prolonged periods. I was able to get them to add that note to my record. You will take all these records with you to your SSA appointment. Being in pain is not sufficient. You must have provable conditions that keep you from standing, walking, sitting. Is there some job you can do even if it is way less money than you are used to making? Remember, money doesn't matter. I was making $94,000 annually before I stopped working. If it could be shown I could sit at a desk for 8 hours at $8.00 per hour that's what they would tell me to do. So everything you speak of keep in mind to reply so that you are not giving any leeway to pigeon hole you into a job. This does not mean lie. If you are able to work you should work. Now there are factors SSA uses to consider your life skills, education, and age and how likely it is you could find work. I can only tell you my situation was I had earned in my work career enough to qualify for disability payments and I did not apply for SSI, only SSDI. So your circumstances will dictate what you apply for but filling out the forms is the same.

Chapter Five

The application is mostly just information and is straight forward. As I mentioned earlier you will be able to work on this ..stop…come back and pick up where you left off. Okay, very important you will list your physical and mental conditions. If you meet the "listing" put that on here. To learn what the listings are go to https://www.ssa.gov/disability/professionals/bluebook/AdultListings.htm .

The way I read their website is that meeting a listing is automatic approval. I felt that I met the listing so if you do also when listing your conditions refer to the listing number so it calls the examiners attention to it. Here is exactly what my application had on it.

Conditions

List of physical and mental conditions:

1. Listing 1.02 a bilateral knee OA bone on bone
2. Listing 9.00b5 Diabetes typed 2 uncontrolled

3. Morbid Obesity
4. Hypertension
5. Evolving Leukocytoclastic vasculitis
6. Sciatica- numbness in thigh for over 1 year
7. Sleep Apnea

And I had all the medical records to back this up. Some of these I know had no issue of preventing me from working but I figured it was best to list everything to paint the entire picture.

The next thing is all of your doctors and their info but pay careful attention when describing your medical conditions. You want to make sure you describe them in a way that explains why you can't do ANY job. Here is mine regarding my knees which is what put me out of commission from working.

Medical Conditions Treated: "Osteoarthritis. According to my doctor both of my knees are bone on bone. I am unable to stand or walk without severe pain that increases with the duration. The longer I try to stand, the pain and stiffness increases. I cannot concentrate or focus because all of my attention is focused on getting off my feet. Once I sit down it helps the pain and I need to extend my legs to help alleviate the stiffness. If I sit for more than 20 minutes I become stiff and the pain starts and the longer I sit the worse it gets. It is difficult to arise from the seated position and when I do I am extremely stiff and I need to move about a little to get moving again. "

So I painted a very clear picture of my problem where standing, walking and sitting keep me from doing any reasonable job. As you can imagine an employer even in a sit down job would not tolerate me having to get up every 15 or 20 minutes and walk a little essentially taking a large number of breaks. This is how you need to describe your issues. Do it in ways that explain why you can't work. You will do this in the job details as well as in the additional information section. Again be truthful. Here is my Additional information that I filled out on my application.

"My knees are adversely effecting my life. I am unable to walk without severe pain as I am bone on bone. If I am on my feet I am in pain and it becomes more and more severe the more I walk. My knees become very stiff and I can't tolerate more than about 30 minutes. Even when I sit down after walking I need to extend my legs to alleviate the stiffness. My orthopedic doctor says I have no cartilage left and I am bone on bone. Standing is even worse than walking. I cannot stand more than 3 or 4 minutes without pain and the longer I stand the worse it gets. If I stand for 30 minutes I am desperate to get off my feet and can't concentrate because the pain is all I think about. Once I do sit down I must extend my legs to move them and alleviate the stiffness. Sitting for an extended period (30 minutes) makes my knees get stiff and I have the need to extend them and get up and walk around just enough to alleviate the stiffness and then sit down before the pain gets to great from walking or standing. My everyday activity is effected such as shaving, showering, cooking, doing laundry, toileting, using stairs are all altered to keep me from being on my feet. I can drive a car but the stiffness, just like sitting in a chair, gets bad after about 30 minutes. When I get out of the car it is difficult to straighten my legs so it takes a little bit to get moving again. If I am in a situation where I am forced to sit for prolonged period (an hour or more) I am so stiff and in pain to the degree I can't think about anything else. It makes it very difficult to focus. I live my life in segments of how to obtain relief. Walk a little, stand a little, sit a little. My mind is always occupied with getting relief. My out of control diabetes and my obesity are not helping. I am short of breath if I walk to my car which is only 100 feet. I am constantly trying to watch what I eat and have had some success but gained it back. Please give me your utmost consideration. "

So this takes care of the application and you are ready to submit. You need to tailor it to your specifics, be truthful, and don't just copy what I did. Make it your own.

Remember to spell out the listing, paint the picture of how it keeps you from working.

Chapter Six

The appointment. I arrived with everything I was told to bring and I was called to the window. It did not take very long at all once they opened the doors. I arrived about thirty minutes early before they opened but they don't open the doors until 9:00 am. Now here is the strange part. The girl I was talking too said she was surprised I was even there because I filed online. She said I was told wrong but this may have been a blessing in disguise. This young lady took my medical files and nothing else. Because I did not file for SSI, only SSDI none of the rest was needed. She did ask me a couple of questions about work history and that was it. She was extremely nice and told me the next step my files would go to Disability Determination Services. This is actually located in another city but still in my state. She said all my medical files would be scanned in and anything else they needed they would be in touch. They would request any medical information needed from my doctors. Let me give you a hint: be very polite. You will gain nothing being contrary and rude. This young lady could not have been any nicer to me. So now I wait. I would like to say I patiently waited but I checked my status online many times every day. I was a wreck as I am sure you will be also. Remember the only thing in this step is making sure you even qualify based on earnings to get disability. This office does not make a determination based on medical evidence, that is done by DDS.

Chapter Seven

Within a week I received some forms to fill out by hand and you MUST have them returned on time or you will be denied. It is the Adult Function Report. It asks similar questions as the initial application so just fill them out with the same thought in mind- how it keeps you from working. Keep a copy of this form before you sign it. This way if it gets lost you can sign it and rush it to them. Don't think if your late they will care why. You will be denied. I called the Disability Examiner two days before it was due to make sure she had it. Her phone number will be on the letter you get. You will probably have to leave a message and be sure to leave your case number. It is on your letter. The examiner confirmed to me she had it and would contact me if she needed anything else. Now you are officially done. Just wait and sweat bullets. When you go online to check your status you will see a message that states what step you are on. For me it said step 2 of 3. Everything online said there are 5 steps. I tried everywhere to find out why mine said 2 of 3. I wondered if it meant I only had 3 steps because I met the "listing". I was never able to figure this out but in the end it said 3 of 3 and I assume it was for that reason. I made three calls to the disability examiner. One after about 2 weeks and she told me it was being processed and gave me the company line that the initial application usually takes about 3 months. I called at 31 days and just checked again because the online status said a medical decision had been reached. The examiner told me she couldn't tell me anything because they go for review and it could be reversed. She did tell me I could call back the next day if I haven't heard anything. I did not hear anything so I called again. She told me she couldn't tell me the verdict but stated I would be happy with the conversation when SSA contacted me. I was ecstatic because she essentially told me I got it. Again, this examiner was extremely nice every time I talked to her. I received the back pay about a week later and a letter in about two weeks. SSA never did call me but I am receiving monthly benefits. So that is the story of how I was approved for SSDI in 32 days.

Chapter 8

I don't know if you will have the same success I did but in my entire experience the SSA and DDS were so kind and professional they dispelled the myth that is being perpetuated online. My guess is many people don't put forth the effort on the initial application or aren't really qualified for disability. If forms are not filled out in their entirety or properly or if deadlines are missed you will likely be denied. I wish all of you the best and I hope this little book may help you in your journey. Always be kind to those you are dealing with and good luck.

70636325R00017

Made in the USA
Lexington, KY
14 November 2017